POND LIFE

POND LIFE

PHOTOGRAPHED BY
FRANK GREENAWAY

WRITTEN BY
BARBARA TAYLOR

A FUNFAX BOOK

A FUNFAX BOOK

Project editor Christiane Gunzi **Art editor** Val Wright Heneghan

Editorial assistant Deborah Murrell **Designer** Julie Staniland
Design assistant Nicola Rawson

Production Louise Barratt
Illustrations Nick Hall, Nick Hewetson, Dan Wright
Additional editorial assistance Jill Somerscales

Managing editor Sophie Mitchell
Managing art editor Miranda Kennedy

Consultants
Barry Clarke, Theresa Greenaway,
Paul Hillyard, Mandy Holloway, Kathie Way

Pond snail's radula, p.28 photographed by John Cooke,
Oxford Scientific Films, Ltd.
Endpapers photographed by Eckart Pott, Bruce Coleman Ltd.

FunFax is an imprint of Covent Garden Books Ltd.,
95 Madison Avenue, New York NY 10016

Visit us on the World Wide Web at
http://www.dk.com

Copyright © 1998 Covent Garden Books Ltd., London

Paperback edition, 1998
2 4 6 8 10 9 7 5 3 1

ISBN 0-7894-2970-5

Color reproduction by Colourscan, Singapore
Printed and bound in Singapore by Imago

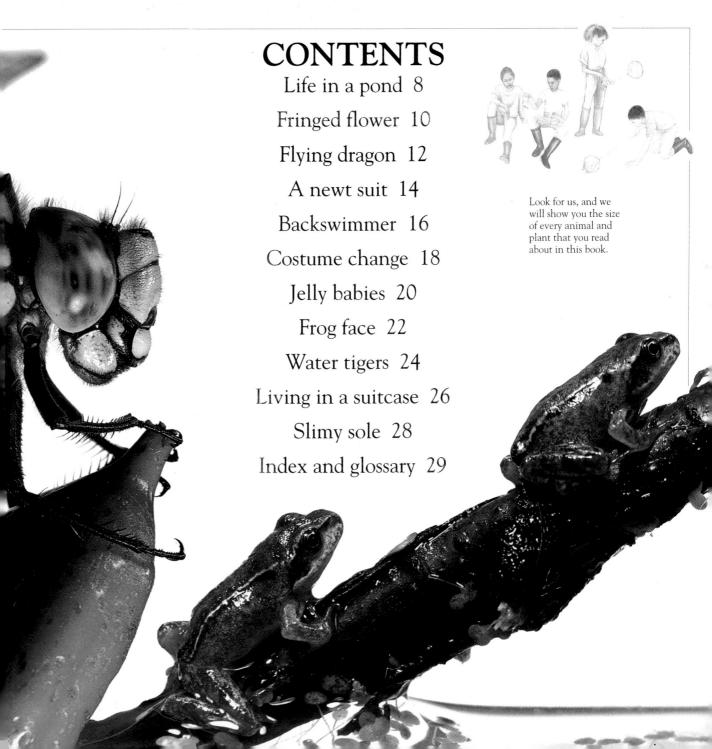

CONTENTS

Look for us, and we will show you the size of every animal and plant that you read about in this book.

LIFE IN A POND

THE STILL WATER OF A POND is a miniature world that is easily upset by changes such as drought conditions and pollution. Pond plants provide food and shelter for all kinds of insects, spiders, and amphibians. Some plants, such as water lilies, float on the water's surface. Frogs start their lives in the water as spawn (eggs), then become tadpoles, climbing out onto the land when they are young adults. Many insects begin life in the water as eggs. They take to the air when they become adults and return to the pond later to breed.

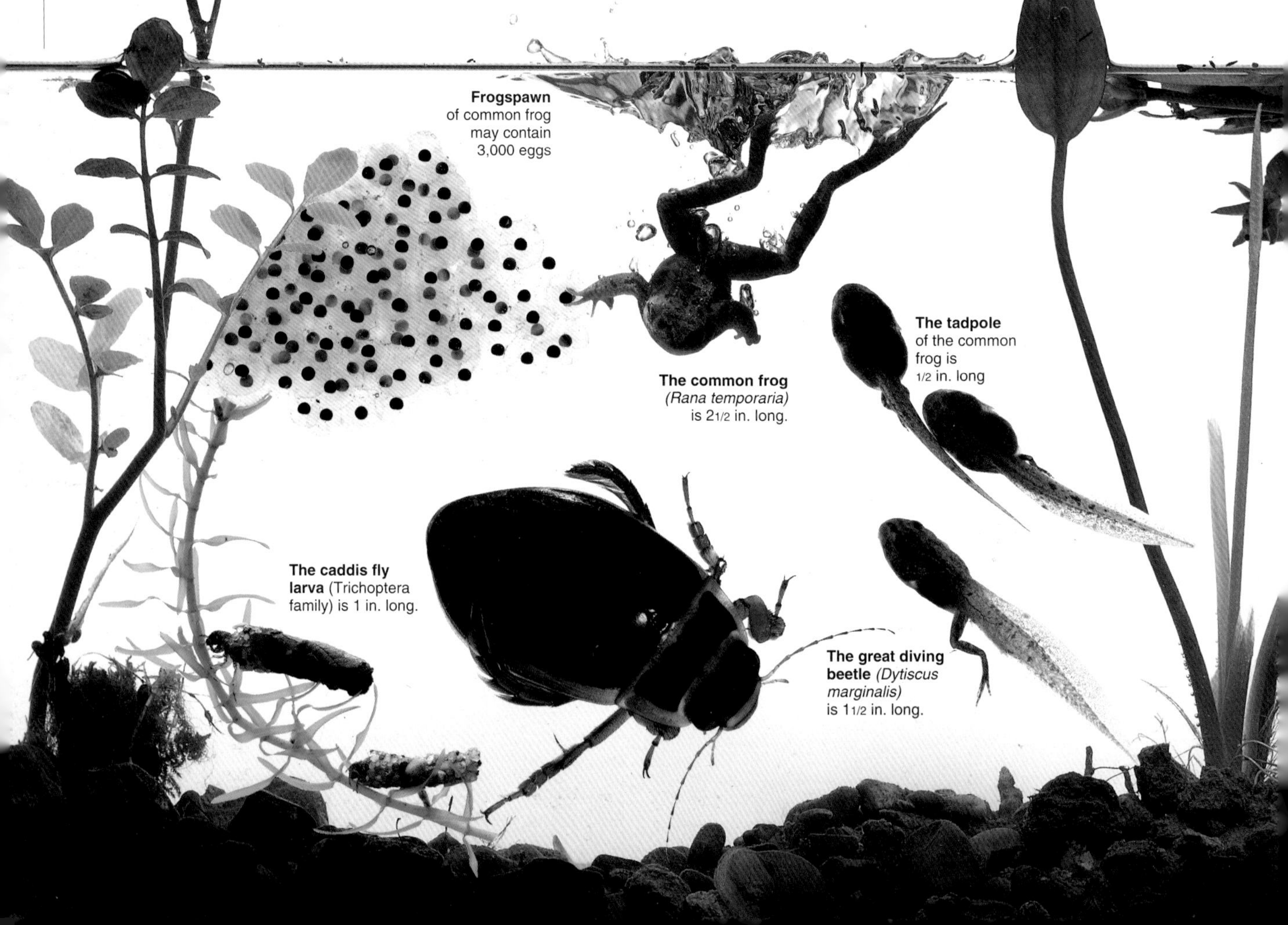

Frogspawn
of common frog
may contain
3,000 eggs

The common frog
(*Rana temporaria*)
is 2 1/2 in. long.

The tadpole
of the common
frog is
1/2 in. long

**The caddis fly
larva** (Trichoptera
family) is 1 in. long.

**The great diving
beetle** (*Dytiscus
marginalis*)
is 1 1/2 in. long.

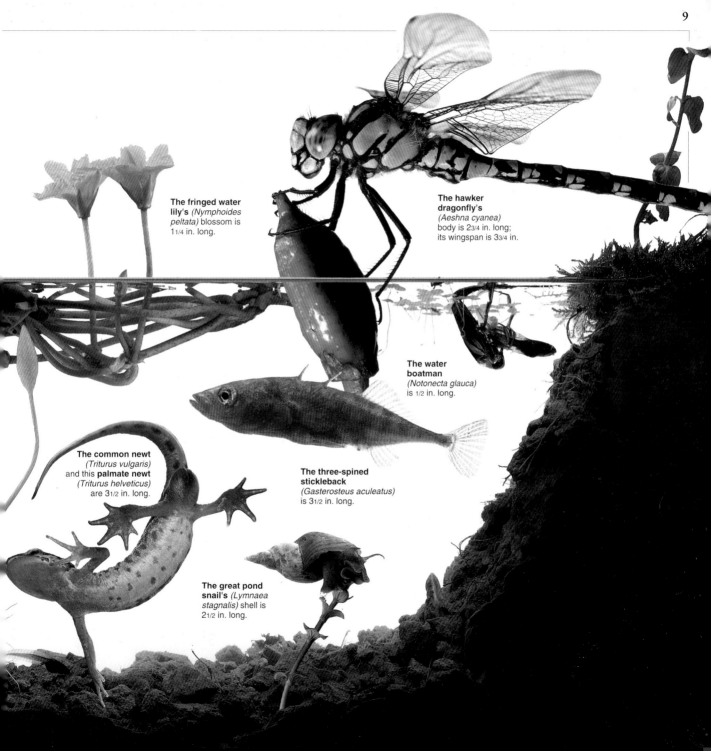

The fringed water lily's *(Nymphoides peltata)* blossom is 11/4 in. long.

The hawker dragonfly's *(Aeshna cyanea)* body is 23/4 in. long; its wingspan is 33/4 in.

The water boatman *(Notonecta glauca)* is 1/2 in. long.

The common newt *(Triturus vulgaris)* and this **palmate newt** *(Triturus helveticus)* are 31/2 in. long.

The three-spined stickleback *(Gasterosteus aculeatus)* is 31/2 in. long.

The great pond snail's *(Lymnaea stagnalis)* shell is 21/2 in. long.

FRINGED FLOWER

THE FLAT LEAVES of water lilies float on the pond like heart-shaped saucers. The fringed water lily is named that because its yellow flowers have fringed edges. Its leaves provide shade and shelter for many fish and other pond creatures hiding from enemies or waiting for a meal. Animals such as snails eat the leaves or lay their eggs on them. The leaves also produce food for the plant. The water lily stores some of this food in a thick stem under the water called the rhizome, to help it survive the winter. The rhizome is anchored in the mud at the bottom of the pond. Inside the plant, there are air spaces to keep it upright and floating. These air spaces contain oxygen, which the fringed water lily uses to release energy from its food in order to grow.

GUESS WHAT?
Although the fringed water lily looks like a true water lily, it is more closely related to blue flowers called gentians, which grow on mountains.

The leaves have a waxy surface so that water runs off them easily. This helps to stop them from getting waterlogged.

In cold or rainy weather, the flowers may stay closed to protect the pollen inside.

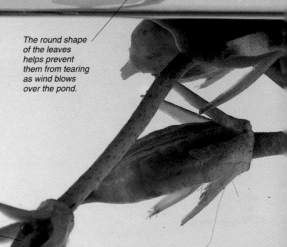

The round shape of the leaves helps prevent them from tearing as wind blows over the pond.

FLOATING FRUITS
After flowering, the stems bend down over the pond so that the egg-shaped fruit can develop under the water. Each fruit contains seeds that develop once the flower has been pollinated by an insect. The fruit eventually floats away from the parent plant and grows into a new water lily if it lands in a suitable place.

After flowering, each flower head becomes a fruit that develops under the water.

A LIGHT MEAL
The water lily's leaves use the energy in sunlight to make food for the plant. Each floating leaf has breathing pores called stomata on the top surface, rather than underneath, as in land plants. This is so that the gases needed for breathing and making the food can pass between the air and the inside of the leaf.

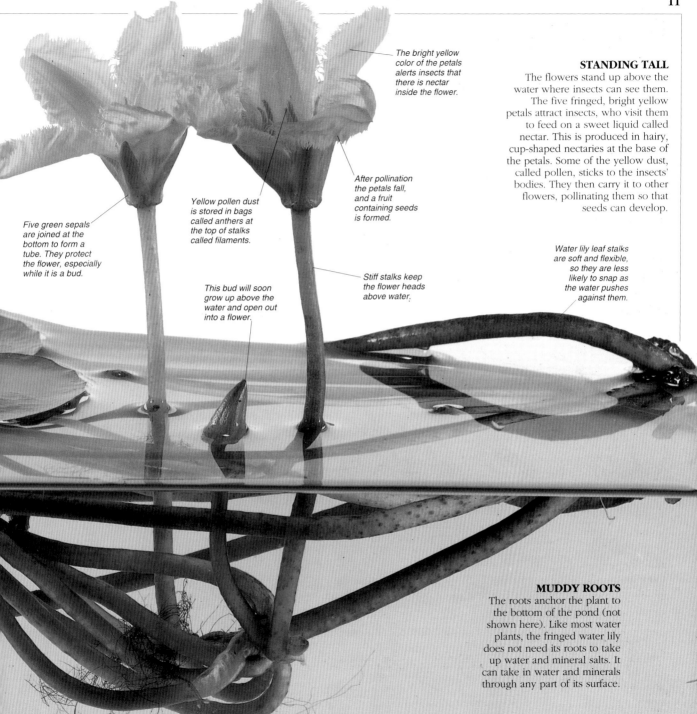

The bright yellow color of the petals alerts insects that there is nectar inside the flower.

After pollination the petals fall, and a fruit containing seeds is formed.

Yellow pollen dust is stored in bags called anthers at the top of stalks called filaments.

Five green sepals are joined at the bottom to form a tube. They protect the flower, especially while it is a bud.

This bud will soon grow up above the water and open out into a flower.

Stiff stalks keep the flower heads above water.

Water lily leaf stalks are soft and flexible, so they are less likely to snap as the water pushes against them.

STANDING TALL

The flowers stand up above the water where insects can see them. The five fringed, bright yellow petals attract insects, who visit them to feed on a sweet liquid called nectar. This is produced in hairy, cup-shaped nectaries at the base of the petals. Some of the yellow dust, called pollen, sticks to the insects' bodies. They then carry it to other flowers, pollinating them so that seeds can develop.

MUDDY ROOTS

The roots anchor the plant to the bottom of the pond (not shown here). Like most water plants, the fringed water lily does not need its roots to take up water and mineral salts. It can take in water and minerals through any part of its surface.

FLYING DRAGON

THE LARGE POWERFUL WINGS of the dragonfly help
it zoom backward and forward over the pond with lightning
speed, like a tiny helicopter. About 300 million years ago,
there were dragonflies with wings as big as gulls' wings,
but the dragonflies that live today are only the size
of large butterflies. The dragonfly's wings beat up
and down about 20 times per second, pushing it
along at up to 20 miles per hour. This allows it
to catch fast-flying insects and escape from
birds and other predators. Dragonflies mate
above the pond, then lay their eggs on water
plants. The eggs hatch into nymphs that
live underwater for several years. They are
fierce hunters, grabbing water insects and
young fish. Eventually, the nymphs evolve
into adult dragonflies with wings and leave
the water to begin their life in the air.

*Each foot has two
hooks for holding
onto slippery
surfaces.*

HAWK EYE
Giant, bulging eyes cover
most of the dragonfly's head.
Each eye has up to 30,000
separate sides called lenses.
These lenses can detect
moving objects up to
66 feet away.

*Because dragonflies have
excellent eyesight, they
only need these two tiny
feelers, called antennae,
for smelling things.*

*Tiny hairs
on each leg
help the
dragonfly to
grip its prey.*

*These strong
jaws called
mandibles are
sharp and pointed
for tearing food
into tiny pieces.*

*Each leg has
joints, so it can
bend easily.*

FAST FOOD
Dragonflies hold their
legs forward like a net
to scoop up gnats and
other flying insects.
Sometimes they also
catch bees and wasps.
Dragonflies usually
munch their meals while
they are flying.

SPIKY LEGS
Rows of spikes on
each leg help the
dragonfly to hold
onto slippery surfaces
and keep a grip on its
food. The legs are right at
the front of the body, just
behind the mouth. This makes it easy
to grasp things but difficult to walk.

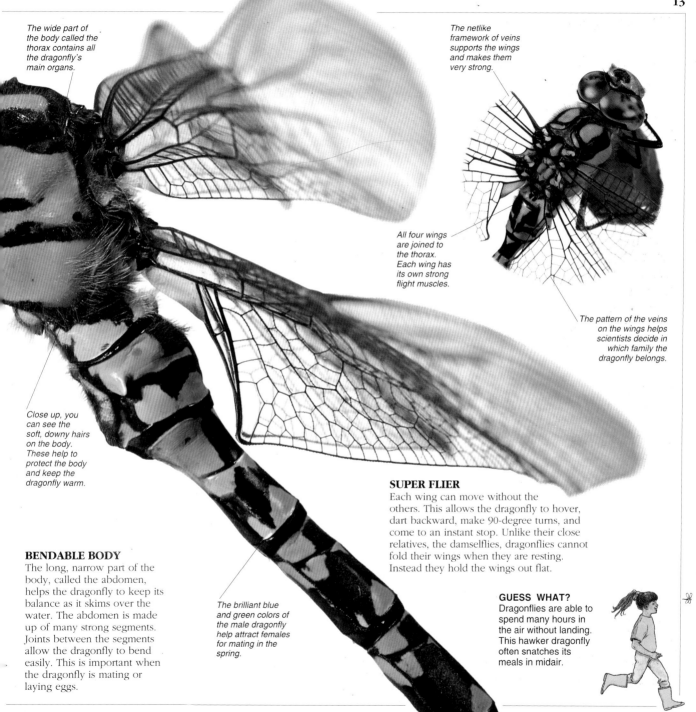

The wide part of the body called the thorax contains all the dragonfly's main organs.

The netlike framework of veins supports the wings and makes them very strong.

All four wings are joined to the thorax. Each wing has its own strong flight muscles.

The pattern of the veins on the wings helps scientists decide in which family the dragonfly belongs.

Close up, you can see the soft, downy hairs on the body. These help to protect the body and keep the dragonfly warm.

SUPER FLIER

Each wing can move without the others. This allows the dragonfly to hover, dart backward, make 90-degree turns, and come to an instant stop. Unlike their close relatives, the damselflies, dragonflies cannot fold their wings when they are resting. Instead they hold the wings out flat.

BENDABLE BODY

The long, narrow part of the body, called the abdomen, helps the dragonfly to keep its balance as it skims over the water. The abdomen is made up of many strong segments. Joints between the segments allow the dragonfly to bend easily. This is important when the dragonfly is mating or laying eggs.

The brilliant blue and green colors of the male dragonfly help attract females for mating in spring.

GUESS WHAT?

Dragonflies are able to spend many hours in the air without landing. This hawker dragonfly often snatches its meals in midair.

A NEWT SUIT

NEWTS ARE SHY, SECRETIVE animals. For part of the year, they live on land, hiding out of sight under cool, moist rocks or leaves. They come out at night to feed on worms, slugs, insects, and snails. In winter, newts usually hibernate (sleep) in cracks in the ground or under rocks or the bark of dead trees. The fat stored in their bodies helps them stay alive during the coldest months. In spring, they return to the ponds and their skin becomes thinner and easier to breathe through for their life under water. They court one another, mate, and lay eggs. The eggs hatch into carnivorous (meat-eating) young called tadpoles. Newt tadpoles have feathery gills to take in oxygen from the water so that they can breathe. By the fall, the young have developed into tiny versions of the adults. They leave the pond and live on land until they are ready to breed.

The skin allows water to pass through it, so the newt has to live in a damp place or it will dry out and die.

Special glands in the skin produce a slimy mucus to keep the newt's body smooth and moist. This also helps the newt escape from predators, by simply sliding out of their grasp.

Ridges develop along the sides of this newt's body in the spring.

COURTSHIP COLORS

This male common newt develops a speckled orange belly when he is ready to mate. His bright new clothes help to attract a female. In winter, the skin turns back to a dull brown color. The bright colors are also a sign that the newt tastes horrible. They warn predators to leave it alone.

SWIMMING TAIL

During the breeding season, the male's tail becomes flattened to help him do a courtship dance in the water for the female. Some male newts also develop ridges along the sides of the body and a short hairlike filament at the tip of the tail. The newt shakes the end of the tail to push water along the ridges. The water picks up scent from glands in the newt's skin and carries it toward the female.

In the breeding season, special organs develop in the skin. They are sensitive to vibrations in the water and help the newt find a mate.

The eyes are on top of the head for spotting prey. They can easily locate small animals in the pond if they are moving.

GUESS WHAT?
Newts migrate long distances to find a suitable place to breed. They often travel to the pond where they grew up, finding their way by sight and smell.

These webbed back feet allow the palmate newt to swim extra fast.

Every few weeks, this newt molts. Newts sometimes eat the empty skin once it has peeled off their body.

Close up, you can see tiny veins under the skin. They carry blood full of oxygen around the body.

FLIPPER FEET
Most palmate newts develop webbed back feet in the breeding season. These act as flippers and help them to swim faster than the females, so they can do their courtship dance.

BACKSWIMMER

WATER BOATMEN ARE so named because they look like tiny boats rowing across the pond. Their strong back legs look like the oars. These insects are also called backswimmers because they swim on their backs. Water boatmen have wings and can fly. They are fierce hunters with large appetites and attack creatures much larger than themselves. In spring, the female lays cigar-shaped eggs, pushing them into the stems of water plants. After several weeks, white larvae with red eyes hatch out of the eggs. They are shaped like the adults but have no wings and spend much of their time at the bottom of the pond. By late summer, after molting several times, they develop into winged adults.

Claws on each leg help the insect hang upside down from the surface of the water or grip onto objects under the water.

The back curves inward and downward like the keel underneath a boat.

The tip of the abdomen breaks through the surface of the water to take in air.

Long bristles make the back legs paddle-shaped and help the insect swim quickly.

Each back leg has powerful muscles for swimming.

Large compound eyes help the insect spot its prey.

ROWING BOAT
The water boatman has a streamlined, boat-shaped body. The long, powerful back legs are flattened and fringed with hairs. They stick out of the side of the body, like oars, for rowing the insect through the water. When the water boatman stops swimming, it often holds onto something under the water. If it doesn't, the air trapped under its wings will make it float to the water's surface.

HAIRY SIDE UP
Water boatmen take in air from the surface through two breathing holes called spiracles found at the end of the abdomen. They also store air beneath the wings and between thick hairs under the body. The air trapped under the water boatman's body tips the insect onto its back. This is why it usually swims upside down.

GUESS WHAT?
Although they look like beetles, water boatmen are a kind of water bug. They belong to a group of animals whose scientific name is *Hemiptera*.

FLOATING FOOD
A tiny plant called duckweed often forms a carpetlike mass on the surface of a pond. It floats free in the water with its roots hanging down and provides food for snails, insect larvae, fish, and ducks.

Duckweed floats on the surface of the water.

Smooth, hard wing cases protect the strong flying wings underneath.

The sharp mouthparts pierce the tadpole's flesh, then suck out the liquids inside.

These legs are jointed so that the insect can fold them out of the way when flying.

DEADLY BITE
The water boatman can give a human finger a painful bite. Despite its small size, it eats tadpoles and small fish, as well as underwater insects. It also snaps up moths and other insects from the surface of the pond. The water boatman holds its prey with its front legs and injects toxic (poisonous) saliva with its mouthparts. Then it sucks up the body fluids of its victim.

COSTUME CHANGE

THE STARTLING COLORS of this male stickleback last only through the breeding season. Three-spined sticklebacks like this one live in shallow, clean water, where there is plenty of food to eat. Sticklebacks eat almost anything they can catch, including insects, larvae, shrimp, and small fish. In spring, the male stickleback builds a nest on the bottom of the pond. His bright colors attract a female, who lays her eggs in the nest. For about two weeks, the male protects the eggs and young from mammals, birds, and other fish. The young feed on water fleas and tiny worms. They take about a year to develop into adults.

Sharp spines make this fish almost impossible to swallow.

FIERCE FISH

This male three-spined stickleback is so named because of the three sharp spines on his back. He raises the spines to make himself look more fierce and to scare enemies away from his territory. There are also spines on the underside of the body. When they are all raised, it is very difficult for a larger fish to swallow the stickleback.

COLOR CODE

In spring, the male stickleback develops a deep red throat and chest, bright blue eyes, and silvery scales on his back. These bright colors act like a code to tell females that he is looking for a mate. They also warn other males to keep out of his territory. This is where his nest is, and it is something he fiercely defends.

Colorful eyes attract a mate.

GUESS WHAT?

In the breeding season, male sticklebacks attack any red object, even if it is not a fish, because they think it may be another male threatening their nest.

The stickleback has a blunt snout, which it uses to dig a hollow for its nest.

WATERY HOME

The male stickleback builds an underwater nest for his young. He finds a site, then clears a hollow in the gravel with his snout. Next, he carries bits of plants to the site in his mouth. He produces a special sticky liquid in his body and then uses his mouth to glue the bits together. Sticklebacks usually build their nests in calm water, fixing them to weeds or rocks. Because the young need plenty of oxygen to grow, the male uses his fins to wave lots of clean, oxygen-filled water over them.

The stickleback uses its small mouth for carrying plants to the nest site.

The spines fold flat against the body when they are not needed.

The tail fin moves from side to side to push the fish through the water.

The underbelly turns red in the breeding season.

Gills on each side of the head take in oxygen from the water. They are protected by a hard cover called an operculum.

A long, streamlined body allows the stickleback to swim fast and escape from enemies.

FADED GLORY

The male stickleback's bright colors fade after the breeding season. He becomes a dull brownish yellow, like the female. This dull color camouflages the fish and helps protect it from enemies, such as perch and pike.

JELLY BABIES

IN THE SPRING, adult frogs dive into the pond to breed. They are excellent swimmers, with powerful back legs and webbed feet. The male croaks loudly to attract a female for mating. As soon as the female releases her eggs into the water, the male fertilizes them so that they will develop into tadpoles. At first, the eggs (frogspawn) sink to the bottom of the pond, surrounded by a layer of jelly. Soon the jelly swells with water, and the frogspawn floats to the surface. About two weeks later, tadpoles hatch out. They breathe using feathery gills on their heads. After five weeks, the outside gills disappear and the tadpoles develop lungs inside their bodies. Soon the back legs begin to grow and the tadpoles swim to the surface of the pond to breathe air. Many tadpoles are eaten by diving beetles and newts. This is why frogs lay so many eggs. At least some tadpoles will survive to develop into adults.

The eyes and nostrils are on top of the head, so the frog can see and breathe while most of its body is underwater.

SUPER SWIMMER
The long, thin body and rounded snout give the adult frog a streamlined shape for swimming fast. Adult frogs are very shy and leap into the water to hide at the first sign of danger.

The frog comes to the surface to gulp air down into its lungs. It can also breathe through its skin.

Now that this frog is fully grown, it is old enough to find a mate and breed.

In the breeding season, the male will develop rough, swollen pads, called nuptial pads, on his fingers. These nuptial pads help him to grip the female's slippery body during mating.

TAPIOCA PUDDING
Large clumps of frogspawn float on the surface of the pond. Frogspawn consists of hundreds of tiny, round eggs and looks sort of like tapioca. The transparent jelly protects the eggs from damage caused by other animals and the movement of the water. It also helps prevent molds and microscopic creatures from feeding on the eggs.

GUESS WHAT?
Frogs lay up to 3,000 eggs at one time. The jelly around the eggs helps to keep them warm. The temperature inside a cluster of eggs is often much higher than the temperature of the pond water around them.

Webbed feet are like flippers and help the frog push against the water to swim quickly away from danger.

Under the water, the eyes are protected by an extra transparent eyelid, called a nictitating membrane.

TADPOLE TERRORS
Tadpoles have fleshy lips with rows of teeth for eating water plants. By the time a tadpole is seven weeks old, it also eats dead animals in the pond. Sometimes tadpoles even eat one another.

At twelve weeks old, tadpoles look like tiny frogs but they still have a tail. The tail eventually disappears altogether.

Tadpoles swim by wriggling their long tails.

When the tadpoles first hatch out, they have gills outside the body to take in oxygen from the water.

At five weeks old, a tadpole has legs.

FROG FACE

IN THE MIDDLE OF SUMMER, hundreds of tiny young frogs leave the pond to begin their adult lives on land. Like many other amphibians, these common frogs spend their adult lives in damp, grassy places. Their long back legs and slim, streamlined shape allow them to leap away to escape predators. Large bulging round eyes help them spy their food of insects, slugs, and snails. It takes three years for a young frog to grow into an adult and return to the pond to breed. In fact, frogs often return to the place where they first hatched from frogspawn, but no one knows how they find their way there.

LOOK OUT

The large eyes bulge out of the top of the head, so the frog can keep a sharp look out for food and danger. The eyes are very sensitive to movement, such as an insect flying past. When frogs leap, they often draw their eyes back into their sockets to protect them from damage.

Each eye has special glands that produce moisture to stop it from drying out.

Frogs have good hearing. Just behind the eye is a large eardrum, which leads to the rest of the ear inside the head.

COAT OF MANY COLORS

The colorful patterns on the frog's skin help to camouflage it from enemies such as rats, herons, and grass snakes. A frog can also make its skin become darker to match its surroundings. This color change takes about two hours.

Patterns on the frog's skin help to disguise it in the grass.

Nostrils for breathing air when the frog is on the land

There are small, sharp teeth inside the mouth, which help the frog grip its food.

The frog's long tongue is covered with a sticky mucus.

Each time the frog croaks, this loose skin on its throat expands. Frogs make lots of different sounds, especially during the breeding season.

STICKY TONGUE
The frog's long tongue is attached to the front part of the mouth so that it can dart out to catch insects, slugs, and snails. It is covered with a slimy substance called mucus so that food sticks to it. The frog often swallows its food whole, including snail shells.

Many of these young frogs will be eaten by predators before they are fully grown.

BREATHING SKIN
When young frogs climb out of the water and onto the land, they begin to breathe with their lungs. Frogs can also breathe through their smooth, moist skin. During the winter, some frogs hibernate under a rotting log or in the mud at the bottom of the pond, taking in air only through their skin.

Frogs sometimes use their long, thin fingers to scrape dirt off food before eating a meal.

GUESS WHAT?
Frogs are only a half-inch long when they first jump out of the pond, but they can soon leap up to twelve times their own length.

WATER TIGERS

GREAT DIVING BEETLES are fierce, ever-hungry hunters. They beat their broad, hairy back legs to push themselves rapidly through the water in search of prey such as tadpoles and fish. When they stop swimming, they float to the surface of the pond unless they hold onto water plants or stones. This is because they carry a supply of air under their wing cases. The air makes them lighter than water. In spring, the female beetle lays her eggs inside the stems of water plants. The eggs hatch into larvae that are such avid hunters that they are sometimes called water tigers. When the larva is about a year old, it crawls out of the pond and burrows in damp soil, where it changes into a pupa. After about three weeks, the pupa splits and an adult beetle crawls out and heads back to the pond.

Smooth wing cases, called elytra, allow water to flow past easily. The hard wing cases protect the delicate flying wings underneath.

Yellow edges, or margins, on the forewings give the beetle the second part of its scientific name, marginalis.

FEARLESS FIGHTER
Adult great diving beetles grab almost anything that comes within reach. They often attack creatures much larger than themselves, such as frogs. They use their large mandibles (jaws) to tear up their food, then swallow the pieces and digest them inside the stomach.

The abdomen is made up of several sections. It can bend at the joints between the sections. This helps it to draw in an air bubble.

All three pairs of legs are joined to the thorax.

These beetles are devouring a stickleback.

Male beetles have suckers on their front legs.

STICKY LEGS
The male great diving beetle has special suckers on his front legs for holding onto the female during mating. The suckers produce a sticky substance to help the male grip the female's body. Her back is ribbed to make it easier to hold.

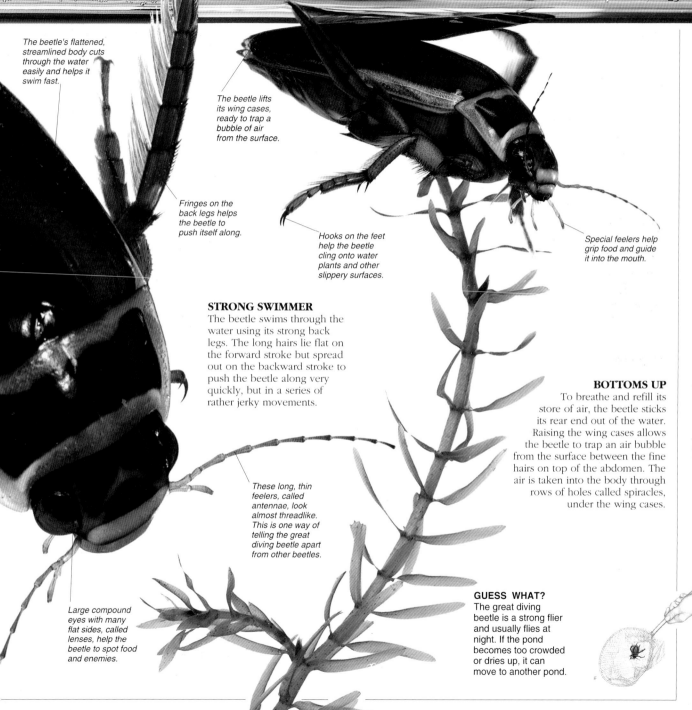

The beetle's flattened, streamlined body cuts through the water easily and helps it swim fast.

The beetle lifts its wing cases, ready to trap a bubble of air from the surface.

Fringes on the back legs helps the beetle to push itself along.

Hooks on the feet help the beetle cling onto water plants and other slippery surfaces.

Special feelers help grip food and guide it into the mouth.

STRONG SWIMMER

The beetle swims through the water using its strong back legs. The long hairs lie flat on the forward stroke but spread out on the backward stroke to push the beetle along very quickly, but in a series of rather jerky movements.

BOTTOMS UP

To breathe and refill its store of air, the beetle sticks its rear end out of the water. Raising the wing cases allows the beetle to trap an air bubble from the surface between the fine hairs on top of the abdomen. The air is taken into the body through rows of holes called spiracles, under the wing cases.

These long, thin feelers, called antennae, look almost threadlike. This is one way of telling the great diving beetle apart from other beetles.

GUESS WHAT?

The great diving beetle is a strong flier and usually flies at night. If the pond becomes too crowded or dries up, it can move to another pond.

Large compound eyes with many flat sides, called lenses, help the beetle to spot food and enemies.

LIVING IN A SUITCASE

WHEN A CADDIS FLY larva (grub) hatches out of its egg in the pond, it builds a long, thin case to hide in. It makes the case from sand grains, leaves, sticks, or small shells. The larva sticks the materials together with silk from its mouth. As the caddis fly larva grows, it makes its case longer by adding new material at the head end. The larva lives in the pond for almost a year before sealing the ends of its case with silk and turning into a pupa. After two weeks, the pupa floats upward and splits as it reaches the surface. The adult emerges, spreads its wings, and flies off. An adult caddis fly survives for about a month and spends most of its short life in the air. During this time, the female lays her eggs in the pond, on stones, or on water plants.

GUESS WHAT?
Caddis fly larvae hold onto their cases with two hooked back legs. They grip it so tightly that they cannot be pulled out without injury.

CARRYING CASE
Each kind of caddis fly larva makes its own special case, using whatever building materials are available. Grappling hooks at the end of the larva's body hold on to the silk lining to keep it firmly inside the case. Three bumps on the first segment of the abdomen also grip the inside of the case. This means the larva can drag its case along as it crawls.

The case is very heavy, so the larva can only move slowly.

Six long legs on the thorax help the larva to pull itself along.

This caddis fly larva has one eye on each side of the head. Some kinds have no eyes at all.

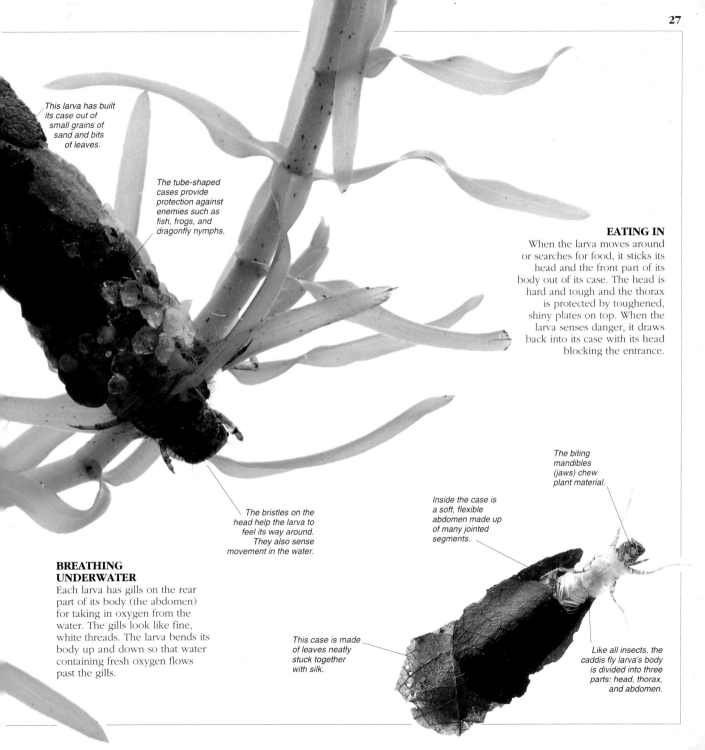

This larva has built its case out of small grains of sand and bits of leaves.

The tube-shaped cases provide protection against enemies such as fish, frogs, and dragonfly nymphs.

EATING IN
When the larva moves around or searches for food, it sticks its head and the front part of its body out of its case. The head is hard and tough and the thorax is protected by toughened, shiny plates on top. When the larva senses danger, it draws back into its case with its head blocking the entrance.

The biting mandibles (jaws) chew plant material.

Inside the case is a soft, flexible abdomen made up of many jointed segments.

The bristles on the head help the larva to feel its way around. They also sense movement in the water.

BREATHING UNDERWATER
Each larva has gills on the rear part of its body (the abdomen) for taking in oxygen from the water. The gills look like fine, white threads. The larva bends its body up and down so that water containing fresh oxygen flows past the gills.

This case is made of leaves neatly stuck together with silk.

Like all insects, the caddis fly larva's body is divided into three parts: head, thorax, and abdomen.

SLIMY SOLE

THE GREAT POND SNAIL glides slowly among the water plants on its large, flat foot searching for food. A hard shell protects the snail's soft body, and when it senses danger, the snail can pull itself back inside the shell for protection. As the snail grows, it makes its shell larger. Pond snails live in water containing a lot of chalk, because they need chalk to build their shells. Pond snails breathe underwater through their skin. They also take in air from the surface of the pond through a special hole in the body. Each snail is both male and female. Usually, two snails meet and fertilize each other's eggs. They lay the eggs in sausage-shaped jelly capsules on water plants or stones. In three to four weeks, the eggs hatch into tiny snails that look just like their parents.

Only the head and foot stick out of the shell. The rest of the snail's body is like a bag coiled up inside the shell.

The snail's shell builds up here.

Snail shells are usually "right-handed." The opening is on the right-hand side of the shell if you hold the shell upright with the opening facing you.

Rows of tiny teeth on the snail's tongue make it look like a nailfile.

BREATHING HOLE
The snail sucks air from the water's surface into its lung through a special breathing hole in the skin. The hole is closed off when the snail is underwater. Air in the lung makes the snail lighter than water, so it floats to the surface unless it holds onto something. When the snail is at the surface, it can push air out of its lung and sink like a stone to escape from danger.

The special tongue for rasping at plants is under the head.

There are glands on the foot that produce a slime called mucus.

SLOW BUT STEADY
The foot of the snail is a large area of muscle. The muscles move in and out in waves. As each wave passes along the foot, the snail moves forward. Special glands produce a slime that helps the foot glide over a surface, so the snail can move at a steady, if not speedy, pace. This snail can also crawl by using small hairs under the foot.

NAILFILE TONGUE
Pond snails, like land snails, have a rough tongue called a radula in their mouth. This has many rows of small teeth to rasp away at food like a nailfile. As the teeth wear down, new ones grow to replace them.

FOOT WITH EYES

The head is at one end of the foot and has two tentacles sticking out of it. The snail cannot draw its tentacles back into its body. They are sensitive to touch and light and help the snail to find its way around.

Each tentacle is flat and pointed and has an eye here, at the base.

GUESS WHAT?

Most pond snails are herbivores (plant eaters), but the great pond snail also eats dead newts and dead fish, and is called a detritus feeder.

The shell is made from chalk in the water. As the snail's body grows larger, it makes its shell bigger too.

The shell has a sharp point called a spire at one end.

The coils on the shell are called whorls.

MOBILE HOME

The shell is a long tube twisted into a series of coils. Each coil is called a whorl. As it grows, the snail adds new whorls that it makes out of chalk from the water around it. The shell acts as a mobile home and protects the body of the snail from enemies.

GLOSSARY

Abdomen *the rear part of the body*
Amphibian *an animal such as a frog, which lives both on land and in water*
Antennae *a pair of feelers*
Carnivorous *meat-eating*
Compound eyes *eyes that consist of many separate lenses*
Elytra *the wing cases of a beetle*
Exoskeleton *a tough covering on the body, made of a substance called chitin*
Detritivore *a living thing that eats dead plants and animals*
Herbivore *an animal that eats plants*
Hibernate *to rest or sleep during the cold months of the year*
Larva *the young, grublike stage of an animal such as an insect*
Mammal *a warm-blooded animal, such as a mouse or rabbit*
Mandibles *jaws*
Migrate *to travel long distances to find food and a suitable place to breed*

Molt *to shed the skin or exoskeleton*
Mucus *a slimy, often poisonous substance which certain animals, such as frogs, produce*
Nymph *the larva of certain kinds of insects, such as dragonflies*
Photosynthesis *the use of sunlight by plants to produce the energy to grow*
Pollen *the dusty powder produced by many flowering plants*
Pollination *transferring the pollen from the male parts of a flower to the female parts of a flower*
Predator *a meat-eating hunter*
Pupa *the resting stage between a larva and an adult insect*
Spawn *a mass of frog's or fish's eggs*
Thorax *the middle part of the body, containing the heart and lungs*
Tentacles *flexible feelers for touching, feeding, or smelling*
Toxic *poisonous*